PROPERTY OF:
NEW HORIZON
1111 SO. CARR
RENTON, WA 9

Sitting Bull

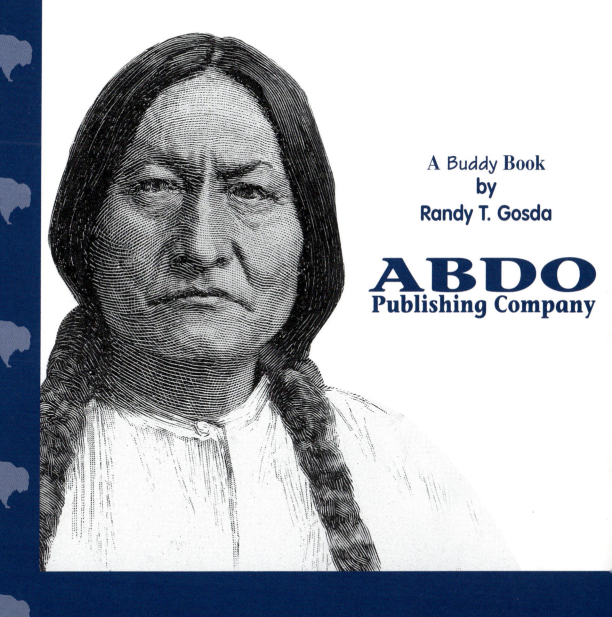

A Buddy Book
by
Randy T. Gosda

ABDO
Publishing Company

VISIT US AT
www.abdopub.com

Published by Buddy Books, an imprint of ABDO Publishing Company, 4940 Viking Drive, Suite 622, Edina, Minnesota 55435. Copyright © 2002 by Abdo Consulting Group, Inc. International copyrights reserved in all countries. No part of this book may be reproduced in any form without written permission from the publisher.

Printed in the United States.

Edited by: Christy DeVillier
Contributing Editors: Matt Ray, Michael P. Goecke
Image Research: Deborah Coldiron, Susan Will
Graphic Design: Jane Halbert
Cover Photograph: North Wind Picture Archives
Interior Photographs/Illustrations: North Wind Picture Archives, Corbis, Library of Congress

Library of Congress Cataloging-in-Publication Data

Gosda, Randy T., 1959-
    Sitting Bull / Randy T. Gosda.
      p. cm. — (First biographies. Set II)
    Includes index.
    Summary: A simple biography of the Souix chief who worked to maintain the rights of Native American people and who led the defeat of General Custer at the Little Big Horn in 1876.
    ISBN 1-57765-737-3
  1. Sitting Bull, 1834?-1890—Juvenile literature. 2. Dakota Indians—Biography—Juvenile literature. 3. Hunkpapa Indians—Biography—Juvenile literature.
  [1. Sitting Bull, 1834?-1890. 2. Dakota Indians—Biography. 3. Hunkpapa Indians—Biography. 4. Indians of North America—Great Plains—Biography.]   I. Title. II. Series Gosda, Randy T., 1959-   . First Biographies. Set II.

E99.D1S6052 2002
978.004'9752—dc21
  [B]

2001034928

Table Of Contents

Who Is Sitting Bull? 4

Young Hunkesi 6

Becoming A Warrior 10

The Wasichus 14

A Broken Promise 18

A Famous Battle 20

Warrior To The End 24

Important Dates 30

Important Words 31

Web Sites 31

Index 32

Who Is Sitting Bull?

Sitting Bull was a great Sioux Indian leader. The Sioux are American Indians. American Indians lived in America before anyone else.

Sitting Bull helped his people win many battles. He was a brave man.

Chief Sitting Bull

Young Hunkesi

Sitting Bull belonged to the Hunkpapa tribe. The Hunkpapa is one tribe of the Sioux nation. They lived on the Great Plains of America.

Sitting Bull was born near the Grand River. Today, this land is South Dakota.

Sitting Bull's tribe lived on the Great Plains.

Sitting Bull was born in 1831. At this time, Sitting Bull's father was the Hunkpapa's chief. A chief is a leader.

Young Sitting Bull's first name was Hunkesi. Hunkesi means slow. Young Hunkesi did not rush. He did things with care.

Hunkesi's tribe hunted buffalo. The Hunkpapa ate buffalo meat. They used the buffalo's skin, hair, and horn, too.

One day, Hunkesi killed a buffalo. He was only 10 years old.

The Hunkpapa hunted buffalo.

Becoming A Warrior

The Hunkpapa warriors fought other tribes. A warrior is someone who fights in a battle. The Hunkpapa warriors fought other Great Plains tribes.

A Native American shield.

When Hunkesi was 14, he followed the Hunkpapa warriors to battle. And young Hunkesi "counted first coup." He was the first of his tribe to strike the enemy. Hunkesi's tribe was proud of him. Hunkesi's father gave him a new name, Sitting Bull.

Young Sitting Bull grew up to be a brave warrior. By 1868, Sitting Bull was chief of the Sioux nation. Chief Sitting Bull was kind and sharing. He loved his people.

The Sioux respected Chief Sitting Bull.

The Wasichus

Over time, other people settled in America. These settlers, or Wasichus, traded with the Hunkpapa tribe. The Hunkpapa let the Wasichus build roads on their land. In return, the Wasichus gave the Hunkpapa goods.

The Wasichus's trains drove the buffalo away.

Over time, the Wasichus's roads drove the buffalo away. Sitting Bull's people needed buffalo to live. The Hunkpapa and the Wasichus started fighting.

Signing the Fort Laramie Treaty.

In 1868, the United States (Wasichus) and the Sioux signed a peace treaty. A treaty is an agreement. The Fort Laramie Treaty set aside land for the Sioux. This land was the Great Sioux Reservation. The Wasichus promised to stay off the Great Sioux Reservation.

A Broken Promise

In 1874, the United States broke the Fort Laramie Treaty. The U.S. went on Sioux land to dig for gold. This gold was in the Black Hills. The U.S. offered to buy the Black Hills from the Sioux. But Sitting Bull did not want to give up his land. The Sioux and the U.S. began fighting again.

South Dakota's Black Hills

Sitting Bull needed help to fight the U.S. So, he met with Chief Crazy Horse. Crazy Horse belonged to another Sioux tribe, the Oglala. Chief Crazy Horse gathered 1,200 warriors to fight the Wasichus. They set up a camp at the Little Big Horn River.

A Famous Battle

George Armstrong Custer was the leader of a U.S. army. On June 25, 1876, Custer's army charged the Little Big Horn camp. Sitting Bull had many more warriors than Custer's small army. Custer and his men lost to the mighty Sioux. This is the famous Battle of Little Big Horn.

Custer's Last Stand is another name for the Battle of Little Big Horn.

Sioux warriors from the Battle of Little Big Horn.

The Sioux won the Battle of Little Big Horn. But the U.S. would not back down. The Wasichus would not leave the Sioux reservation. So, Sitting Bull led his people to Canada in 1877.

Sitting Bull left his home on the Great Plains.

Warrior To The End

At first, Canada was a safe place for Sitting Bull. Then, the buffalo disappeared. Sitting Bull did not want his people to starve. So, he led them back to the U.S. On July 19, 1881, Sitting Bull laid down his rifle. He surrendered to the U.S.

U.S. soldiers keep watch over Sitting Bull and his family.

Sitting Bull quit fighting the Wasichus with guns and arrows. But he never gave up fighting for his way of life.

In 1890, the U.S. tried to take Sitting Bull away from his people. He refused to leave. A fight broke out. A Sioux policeman shot and killed Sitting Bull.

A fight breaks out when Sitting Bull refuses to leave his people.

Sitting Bull's struggle to save his people's way of life is famous. Today, the Sioux are not alone in honoring Sitting Bull. The Wasichus have learned to respect this great warrior.

The Sioux buried their beloved chief in South Dakota.

Important Dates

1831 Sitting Bull is born.

1841 Young Sitting Bull kills his first buffalo.

1844 Sitting Bull becomes a warrior.

1868 Sitting Bull becomes chief of the Sioux nation around this time.

June 25, 1876 The Sioux win the famous Battle of Little Big Horn.

1877 Sitting Bull leads the Sioux to Canada.

1881 Sitting Bull gives up fighting the U.S.

December 15, 1890 Sitting Bull dies in a struggle to stay with his people.

Important Words

American Indians Native Americans, the very first people to live in America.

count first coup to strike the enemy in battle before anyone else.

Great Plains a chunk of flat land in America. South Dakota, North Dakota, Wyoming, and Montana are some Great Plains states.

reservation special land set aside for American Indians.

surrender to give up.

tribe a group of American Indians who live together.

Wasichus an American Indian word for the settlers who came to live in America. The United States people were Wasichus.

Web Sites

New Perspectives on the West
http://www.pbs.org/weta/thewest/
This PBS site is a great source for more information on Sitting Bull and the events of his time.

Custer Battlefield
http://www.intuitive.com/sites/cbhma/index.shtml
Learn more about Sitting Bull and the Battle of Little Big Horn at this site.

Index

American Indian **4**

Battle of Little Big Horn **20-22, 30**

Black Hills **18, 19**

buffalo **8, 9, 15, 24, 30**

Canada **22, 24, 30**

Chief Crazy Horse **19**

Custer, George Armstrong **20, 21**

Custer's Last Stand **21**

Fort Laramie Treaty **16-18**

Grand River **6**

Great Plains **6, 7, 10, 23**

Great Sioux Reservation **17**

Hunkesi **8, 11**

Hunkpapa **6-11, 14, 15**

Little Big Horn River **19**

Oglala **19**

Sioux **4, 6, 12, 13, 17-20, 22, 26, 28-30**

South Dakota **6, 19, 29**

warrior **10-12, 19, 20, 22, 28, 30**